I SOMETIMES FEEL ALONE

By Michael Jacobson

Michael

I SOMETIMES FEEL ALONE
POETRY OF MICHAEL JACOBSON
Copyright 2005 ©Michael Jacobson

ontheedgepress.com

All rights reserved

Printed in the United States of America
No part of this book may be reproduced, copied or used in any manner with out the
express permission of the author.
Fourth Year Dance used with permission.

For information contact: wasunka2@gmail.com
Cover graphics and layout by Chet Lofgren chet.lofgren@studioable.com

DEDICATION

This book is dedicated to the many people I have met, places I have visited, and events that have guided and inspired the words that I write.

A special thank you to River.
A good woman who chooses to stand beside me, despite my many flaws.

To my Step Sons, God-Daughters and Grandchildren;
Chet, Kelly, Kyrrah, Cierra, Miles and Grey.
Your footsteps are steady, strong and your path is clear.
Thank you for allowing me to share the world with you.

To Creator, who makes all things possible.

TABLE OF CONTENTS

FORWARD

This book of poetry embraces a Native American spiritual theme.

These words tell a story.

A few of these poems are deeply personal and even talk of worlds and spirits that only few can sense. Some poems reflect that not all life seems to be respected equally, an unfortunate part of our nature as human beings.

The earth and all of its wonder, including the many creatures that walk, fly, swim, creep and even crawl, have graciously shared their world with us. What do we offer in return?

Michael

I SOMETIMES FEEL ALONE

I sit here in the darkness
Watch the evening stars unfold
Rising far above the mist
From below the forest floor

I'll talk with my Creator
About things I do not know

Of where I might be going
And when that may come true
I'll even question if the answers
Come from me or you

I'll ask you once again
If my prayers – they have been heard
And even as you answer
From your whispers in the dark
Why can't I hear you speak to me?
Why can't I see your spark?

Then I'll finally realize
And that's when you'll lead me home
When I speak and then forget to listen
It's why I sometimes feel alone

TODAY I DID NOT DANCE
(JUNE 28, 1997)

Someone asked the question
But today I did not dance
Even though my heart was ready
Today ~ I had that chance

Inside my thoughts were silent
For the blessing of a friend
There was other work to do
My fear I had to mend

So I let another answer
Before I took that chance

Today ~ I did not dance

I've now had time to sort
The reasons and the why
And when the Tree arose
My heart ~ It sung a cry

But today...

I did not dance

LISTENING

Listen with your heart
It will tell you what direction to take

Walk like the Bear
guiding you step by step
With purpose – treading softly

Hunt like the Wolf
always knowing what to take ~ and when

Listen like the Deer
you will only hear what you need to

Soar like the Eagle
your path will be clear

Listen with your Heart
it will guide you home

LIFE ~ A FRAGILE THING

Held in balance by the air we breathe
The step we take
Only protected
One heartbeat at a time

Only to be lived
by one breath-one step
one heartbeat at a time

Life~ A fragile thing

STORIES

My heart cries-And no one listens
My heart sings-And no one cares
Except...
The Trees
Their soft branches touch me
The Wolf
His mournful songs haunt my own
The Raven
Companion to eternity
The Thunder
Pounding with my heart
The Wind
Whispering my prayers
The soft winter grass ...

These are the spirits
That touch my soul
Caress my heart
And they share with me
Stories that I forget

Tell me once again Grandfather
When the great floods came to this land
When everything we knew was washed clean
The Mother was once again sacred
And the old ways were made easy

CHILDREN'S ROUND

We are the children of the world
Please listen to our plea
We are the children
We stand in unity
We are black - We are white
We are colors of the light
We are all just children of the world

We are the children of the world
Please listen to our plea
We are the children
We stand in unity
We are yellow - We are red
We are colors of the tears we've shed
We are all just children of the world

We are the children of the world
Please listen to our plea
We are the children
We stand in unity
If we all stand together
There's enough for you and me

We are all just children of the world

THE PAINTED ONES

And so-They were sent out across the land.
Their Mother gave them coats to wear
painted them with colors and whispered to each one,
"Your time will come again."

The Painted Ones were sent to the four corners of the earth
and gathered for the people what they needed to survive
When the sun rose once again-
In the West...

EAGLE DANCE

Eagle flying in the sky
Flying up so high
Soaring up above the stars
Eagle – sacred call

Eagle flying in the sky
Flying up so high
Soaring up above the stars
Eagle sees it all

Eagle – Sacred call

Heyoka Bear will tell of darkest things
Of things we do not want to see
Of things we do not want to hear
That we hold very near

~ I M P R I N T S ~

A thousand years ago
The tears of Father sky
Fell to Mother Earth
Leaving imprints buried deep
Scattered far and wide

They are the tears of sadness
They are the tears of joy
Teaching us simplicity
As we begin to understand

Understand the ways of wisdom
Far beyond our fears
Each walking one's own journey
Releasing cleansing tears

Many shadows chase me
None faster than my own
When can I stop running?
For this place that is my home

When I danced
I danced as a child would
In the warmth of the sun
With no one watching

Dancing
With a sadness upon my heart
Feeling the tears of my Mother
As each one fell to the ground

Dancing
Our hearts beating as one

Soon my son ~ soon
You will be free
And the tears and the sadness will be no more

So when that time came
For that bond ~ to be forever broken
The sadness was no more and I too felt the pain
Of bringing life into this world

And the sadness was no more

A DANCER'S PRAYER

Traveling through the night
To a destination known
Following the sun
To find my way back home

Dancing for the children
Young and old alike
Sending out a prayer
To rest in eagle's flight

As we will once again
Find a reason to our rhyme
As we take these sacred steps
These sacred steps in time

O N L Y   O N E

I was in a sacred place
Which only I could be
Where I knew that it was safe
And tomorrow...
would only see

Only I could enter
take a rest from who
I had become
only one would be there
and the heartbeat of the drum

And in this sacred place
You will only find one mirror
As one will often find
it is that ~ you seek to fear

But once you see reflections
You thought forever gone
You speak your peace ~ say your mind
And then...
you sing your song

THE HEARTBEAT

In the distance you will hear it
The callings of a song
And if your heart is listening
The drum will sing along

It is a song of many people
A heartbeat still alive
Through out the many struggles
The spirit will survive

You will feel it in the trees
When you lay upon the earth
On the winds of change
A peaceful sense of worth

Sacred songs of elders
Passed from hand to hand
The heartbeat of one nation
Like the winds of shifting sand

To continue on the journey
Touch each and everyone
And like the peoples' heartbeat
The drum is never silent

The drum is never done

SACRED WAYS

Bear – Eagle – Deer – People
Try as we may – It's never easy
Turtle – Crow – Raven – Creator
Spirit ways
The road – It's path is not always clear
Good people – Bad people – Sacred people
We are all the same
Separate only by the choices we make
But no matter
The fire still burns bright
And the sun will still rise each morning
Does it matter – from which direction?
Sacred ways – Spirit ways – No way
Try as we may – It's never easy
The choice is ours...

WHO WILL TELL

Who will tell the world,
That you were here?
Who will share your stories-speak your name?
as your bones return to the dust of the
Mother

from which you were born
and to which you will return
as your spirit soars ever onward

Who will tell the world,
that you were here?

And the grass will sing a song
Each blade, each stalk, each grain, each seed.
Joining with thousands
Each singing the songs they know
Uniting the world in symphony.

And the people will once again gather
From across the land
To dance beneath the blue sky

Listening to the wind tell the stories of long ago
As it whispers from high above
Caressing the soft green leaves of the New Year

CROW WHO FLIES
(WITH ONE FEATHER MISSING)

It is a reminder
That nothing here is complete
Nothing here is finished
until we finish it

There will always be the one unanswered question
a single thought left undone

it is only then that we realize

the feather is not missing
it never was

imagination
fear
love
hate
envy
truth
lies
honesty
life

it's all there
right where we left it

It is the voice of the people
The heartbeat of a nation
Standing free ~ Standing proud
Bending only to the wind
Bowing only to the dirt beneath their feet
Returning to the center
Only when they learn...

AHU MITAKUYE OYASIN
(ALL MY RELATIONS)

The gathering of the people
Of every nation, and of every creed
Joining within the circle
So that we may spread the seeds

It's more than just the words
Within our prayers and in our deeds
More than just one day
With all we share our needs

We share the songs and learn the ways
The ways of long ago
To rekindle a weakened nation
Now gathering what we've sowed

Once we meet as strangers
But strangers never more
We joined into the circle
To help all spirits soar

The gathering of the people
Many lives, many ways
Come join the sacred circle
Come gather as we say

AHU MITAYUYE OYASIN

Once again
The coyote begins to dance
Come along with me my friend
Step out to embrace the chance
No longer your ties will hold you
No longer does it play the tune
The chains of your bondage are broken
So follow the freedom of wisdom
And the teachings of Grandmother Moon

K O L A   W I
(S U N   F R I E N D)

And when the sun rises
It shall be a new day
What was yesterday shall be left behind

And all the things that have not gone well
Shall be your give-away
And when the sun rises

It shall be a new day

SUN RISE

In every sunrise
There is a heartbeat
Beating strong
Surging, pounding, living
Until that day is done

Each ray a breath of life
In silent golden hue
And in that flash of brilliance
When the day begins anew

A promise

A gift for only you

The promise and a gift
Once again to start brand new
But not forget the path you've been
And what that has done for you

So make this day a golden one
A heartbeat
Beating strong
Surging, pounding, living
Until your days on earth
Your day on earth is done

V I S I O N

My spirit came to visit
In the darkness of this sacred womb
Sharing with me - guidance
And the dance that will come soon

Soon my Grandfather spirits
You'll teach me what I know
What to gather for the journey
And songs that I must know

And in this dance of humbleness
I will honor Mother Earth
To share with her my thankfulness
Continuing the journey
Reclaiming rights of birth

Thoughts go racing through my head
Like thousands of buffalo
Surging across the vast open – endless prairie
Too large to understand
Too large to see
And yet, my eyes strain with all their might to see
What one can never see

And through the pounding thunder
A gentle voice speaks
You must listen with your heart

Walk gently upon the Mother
For she is wounded ~ she is crying
And we have grown deaf

No longer do we hear the wind whispering
through the trees ~ for they are gone

No longer do we feel the life giving blood
flowing through her veins ~ for it now lays stagnant

No longer can we see into her clear blue skies...

What is it that we must do to heal the scars
that now run deeper than our emotions?

How do we ask the wind
to talk to the trees again?
so we can remember how to breathe once more

...dare we ask of the river?
please forgive our ignorance
without your cleansing flow
all life would end

It's really very simple

We must once again

Walk gently upon the Mother
For she is wounded ~ she is crying
And we have grown deaf...

C H A N G E S

I feel the spirits
That walk this land
Of generations past
Shadows of the future
As time now goes by fast

But stories get rekindled
Of where things were back then
Once again the people gather
And the old ways we defend

For some the change is easy
As others take their time
And the seventh generation
Will see the reason to our rhyme

Sounds of thunder and hoof beats
In the whisper of the wind
Returning to what once we knew
Stories learned again

As time once more
And once again
To find where we belong
As we journey in the circle
And the fires burn night long

Emerging into daylight
As evening fades away
Friends and Family gather
One more has found the way

SACRED FIRES

Sometimes it reaches out
And says – I know who you are
Come and sit with me awhile
I know you won't stay long

Come and share the fire
As that too turns to ash
Just memories of forgotten words
Your future is your past

Tell me of your journeys
As the fire burns night long
And I'll share with you some memories
Before they too are gone

And once more as I'm forgotten
As evening fades to day
There will only be a happiness
For we both have found our way

PERHAPS

Perhaps I shall never
find all of me

To retrace every step
ever taken and have
given away

moment by moment
inch by inch
day by day
year after year

Until nothing remains
but the shadow of the
man I used to be

But then the sun
comes once again

and from the shadows
stands a man
I used to be

SACRED DOG LOOKING
(FOR CIERRA)

There is nothing
That the Bear cannot heal
Digging ~ Clawing ~ Swiping
Following spirit
There is nothing
That the Bear cannot heal

And when the sacred Dog
Looks at you
Hey ya wey – Hey ya wey

And when the sacred Dog looks at you
Hey ya wey – Hey ya wey
There is nothing

That the Bear cannot heal

Return-
To your sacred place of prayer
That is all you will ever want
all you will ever be given
all you will ever need
A quiet place
No one owns you
No one owns your life
No one knows your prayer
No one but you
and Creator...

Crow will sing
As Ravens watch from shadows deep

Crow will sing the songs of life
Raven ~ A song of death

Crow will tell of foolish tales
The Raven cannot lie

Crow will greet the morning sun
And Raven ~ The still of night

STORIES II

Faces that you'll never see
That look from shadows deep
Hands that will never touch
Reaching for the stars
These are our stories
And this is our life
As we bury deep our scars

This is the way it must forever be
If we are to protect
The little that is left
And yet - our stories must be told

The ancient ones knew us
They knew who we were
They told our stories
And our songs were sung
But today
Even they are forgotten

And then one day
A child was born
Reaching to the shadows
Looking deep into our eyes

And one by one
Our stories are told
Our songs are sung
And we will once again
Shine as the stars do

Raven flies through shadows
Past the edge of time
Does not stop to ponder
Does not stop to cry
For he will find the shadows...
To ~ no longer chase the rhyme

S K A ' S K A '
(W H I T E   B E A R)

The Bear's growl
Deep
Low
Rumbling
Within...

Healing ~ that which is not seen
Speaking ~ that which is not heard
Feeling ~ that which is not spoken

Deep
Low
Rumbling

Within.
The cave echos...

SPIRIT AND SONG

I'll fly with the spirit of Ravens
Listen to Crows' last song
I must return to my dreams now
For I've been away to long

I must return to my home
Chasing that celestial star
Sit in the dark with animal friends
Feel my mountains caress

Listen to the stories
Of the wind and of the old
The way of battled warriors
And the coming of the cold

I'll cherish the many memories
In the life that I have lived
Do not weep in my passing
For Crow and Raven will give...

Crow will keep the fire
Raven will fight the cold
I'll feel the touch of my loved ones
And cherish growing old

In Crow and Raven ~ You will see my life
Flying high and free
The Crow is in the Raven
And the Raven is in me

SACRED WOMEN

A sacred woman-Standing
Standing proud
Standing tall
Standing humble

Seeking guidance
For the answers
She already knows the questions to

Standing
With knowledge, understanding, compassion...
fear of the unknown facing her
she will turn and welcome
All that Creator has to offer

A sacred woman

Standing...

TAKING LAND

You take this land-like it belongs to you
You come in waves of inhumanity
Leaving behind the things that you did not want anyway
Trampling your way to the next piece of land
That was better than the one you just destroyed

Why do you not see the sickness behind you?
Is it because you have only been taught to look ahead?
Not to the left-Not to the right
Will you not see the shadows that follow you?

Why do you not see footprints other than your own?
Reminders of others that inhabit this land
And when they are gone
Everything that you cherish
Will also disappear

Perhaps it is not too late
Can we find a way to work together?
So those who go before will learn
To support those that follow
And this land will be strong

I HONOR BOTH

I walk a path in two worlds
My spirit honors both

You must look past the color of my skin
My heart beats
With the red blood of my nations
Their songs that are my spirit
Flow through my veins with fire

Songs to tell of origins that go beyond the white sails caressing the ocean blue waves -
I honor both...

The old ones riding through tall prairie grass, carried upon the backs of the sacred
dog - honoring the wind and the sun and the gentle touch of silver raindrops caress-
ing Mother Earth - I honor both...

Guided by the stars - Ancient symbols of ancestors illuminating a path through the
darkness of my sight - I honor both...

The blood of many nations
One Creator

I honor both...

FORBIDDEN LAND

There are things about the east gate
I will never understand
A world within our own
A dark forbidden land

It's where Heyoka dances
Where all wounds go to heal
A place between this world and ours
A cycle of the wheel

But I'll stand there at the threshold
And look with all my might
Scream for my forgiveness
Of the things I will not fight

For spirit has not forgotten
But forgiven what I've done
And all that will be asked of me
Is that fourth day in the sun

RAVEN SONG
(FOR KYRRAH)

Ancient calls of shadows
For the Raven shall now sing
Through the darkness of time
Once a raging heartbeat
Now following gentle rhyme

'Tis not an easy journey
As the fire burns the soul
Standing strong upon your path
Let footsteps guide your spirit
Your heartbeat...
Like the full moon's gentle glow

But when the sun emerges
From shadowed silent night
Let your Raven spirit
Be the first to light the fire
Your heartbeat...

A SACRED PLACE

from the beginning
to the end...
continuing onward-upward
taking with it
all who believe

for these are the ways of our people
of the earth
of the sky
those who live above
those who live below
dancing within the circle of life
the past ~ the present ~ the future

A sacred place

CENTER

There are dark places
That you carry in your heart

You must love them too

For they need to be nurtured
the same as every other
part of your life
so you can remember

Where the center is...

F O U R T H   Y E A R   D A N C E

I danced with half a heart
Part of me was buried like
a gemstone under the wounded
Mother's blanket.

There was a time when my spirit
joined yours, like hawks soaring
on the wind.

I wish I could feel like the
Earth Mother ~ when men in
moccasin feet loved her with
all there heart and spirit.

She was able to give freely then
like a clear dancing stream.

And you could look into her
seeing each other's reflection
dancing on the water.

by River Jacobson

I love you as I have always loved you
And that is forever
No walk upon this earth
No pathway up in Heaven
No raging river thundering down the mountain
Could ever come close to how you make me feel
I love you as I have always loved you
And that is
Forever

SPEAK AS ONE

The spirit that binds our hearts
Speaks in one voice

Our lives are now spent
Honoring the sun
The moon
The stars...
Walking through the silence
And the beauty
Of the forest
Captured by the blue sky
Held in awe - by the power of the trees
Soft grasses tenderly caressing
Our every step

Each footstep is our own
In this path we walk together

Each heartbeat
Softly drumming a rhythm
Telling the story of our lives

The songs of our voices
Speak as one

Illuminated by one light
The stars appear
Silently – one by one
Each singing its own song

The songs of our voices
Speak as one

ALPHA OMEGA

There is only the beginning
There is only the end
And all that is in between
No longer has the same meaning

For we have been told
That all things move with purpose
And it is now that we finally see
It is now that we finally believe

As we now step out of the shadows
And into the light
The light that we have only seen from a distance

All of our wants – our desires – our needs
No longer have the same meaning
For all things move with purpose
There is only the beginning
There is only the end
And all that is in between...

The circle never ends
Touching
Seeing
Feeling
Knowing...

Connected
All at once
In every place
At every time

The circle
Never ends

Made in the USA
Middletown, DE
29 June 2021

43195506R10035